YOUR REASONABLE SERVICE
IN THE LORD'S WORK

PETER MASTERS

SWORD & TROWEL
METROPOLITAN TABERNACLE
LONDON

YOUR REASONABLE SERVICE
IN THE LORD'S WORK

© Peter Masters 1987
Revised booklet edition first published 1994
This edition 2011

SWORD & TROWEL
Metropolitan Tabernacle
Elephant & Castle
London SE1 6SD

ISBN 978 1 899046 08 9

Cover design by Andrew Owen

All rights reserved. No part of this publication may be reproduced or transmitted in any form or by any means, electronic or mechanical, including photocopy, recording, or any information storage and retrieval system, without permission in writing from the publisher.

Printed by Stephens & George, Merthyr Tydfil, UK

Your Reasonable Service
in the Lord's Work

MORE THAN fifty years ago this writer listened to two friends who were explaining to a Roman Catholic how far his church had drifted from real Christianity. They described very vividly various features of that church, such as its pomp and ceremony, the pope and all the priests, monks, nuns, robes, candles, crosses, images, and so on, showing how vastly different all this was from the simplicity of the New Testament church. It was a powerful line of argument, and it certainly made an impression on their listener.

Over the years I have often thought of that event, and wondered how well Bible churches really resemble the churches of New Testament times. Do we accurately reflect the fervour and activity of the early church?

This booklet deals with one major area in which we often fall a long way short of the standard of the Bible. It is a sad fact that there are many Bible-believing Christians who do not engage in any meaningful work for the Lord. They loyally attend the services, and may give fairly generous financial support, but they *do* very little. They appear to be little more than comfortable observers. What do they have in common with the level of activity to which God's people are exhorted in the Bible? We will examine a number of these exhortations in this booklet.

Evangelicals generally have drifted a long way from the concept of 'the working church' which sees the ideal church as one that has every able member being personally active in some avenue of service for the Lord. Some ministers have so despaired of getting near to this that they dismiss it as an impossible ideal, and make little or no effort to organise Christian service opportunities to employ the gifts and energies of their members.

The Lord never intended church members to be like passengers on a bus, just watching the scenery go by and leaving everything to the driver. Neither did he mean us to resemble patients in a hospital, having all our needs attended to by the staff. Some church members these days are like perpetual students, 'ever learning, and never able'. They value doctrinal knowledge, which is fine, but they never graduate and go into employment. They remain as 'hearers only' and spectators. Yet the Bible is full of passages which rebuke head knowledge not matched by committed service for the Lord.

A few years ago a stirring keynote message was preached at the annual rally of a well-known Christian society, and then published in the society's magazine. The theme of the message was how the churches could be revived. It was a masterly unfolding of the need for revival in the churches. But as one read through this, a vital omission became increasingly obvious. There was not a single word of exhortation to believers to *do* anything in the service of the Lord. The speaker appeared to believe that the spreading of the Gospel and the growth of the churches did not depend in any way on believers participating in any witness or work for the Lord. As long as they believed the right things, they could remain 'at ease in Zion', while God caused wonderful things to happen without their involvement.

It is a tragic fact that many believers organise their lives as though the sole calling of Christians is to enjoy hearing the Word of God expounded, to live godly lives, and to look after their families. But we can never be wholly scriptural or spiritual until we take seriously the 'working' words of the New Testament. Every Bible-believing church must try to bring about the total involvement of all fit and able members in the glad service of the Lord, honouring, of course, the voluntary principle. This is not only our duty, but an essential part of our worship also.

Here, then, is an appeal to committed Christians to embrace the biblical concept of *the working church*, and to uphold the old standard by which as many believers as possible are involved in some way in the work and witness of the congregation. We must surely open our minds to the 'work-strive-labour' exhortations of God's Word, taking particular note of the *quality* of effort which these texts demand from us.

We may have assumed that all the Bible's exhortations to committed service for the Lord apply only to people who are apostles, ministers or missionaries. However, *exactly* the same terms are used to describe the labours of 'ordinary' believers. Here we will set out some of these 'working' exhortations grouped into several 'families' of meaning. Are we serving the Lord as we should be? Do we share in the work of the church, shouldering our share of responsibility, participating in the evangelism of adults and children, visiting the community, or taking a role in one of the many other spheres of service? There are so many things to be done, spiritual and practical.

What a millstone it is round the neck of a local church when members do not understand the nature of real commitment, and fail to participate in service. We need look no further than this to explain the decline of sound Christianity, and our weakness at the present time. Listen to the implicit challenge of the strong 'working-striving-labouring' words of the New Testament. How do we match up?

1. The labouring term

In the epistles the Greek term for Christian service most commonly used to describe the service of believers is *kopos*, which means – a striking, beating, or cutting. It calls to mind a labourer chopping something down, scything the harvest, or doing some other heavy manual task. It always indicates laborious toil resulting in the labourer becoming weary and weakened.* This word is employed by Paul when he writes: 'Therefore, my beloved brethren, be ye steadfast, unmoveable, always abounding in the work of the Lord, forasmuch as ye know that your *labour* is not in vain in the Lord' *(1 Corinthians 15.58).* Paul would certainly never have used this word *kopos* to describe a *modest* level of Christian service. He means to say that intensive and tiring service is what the Lord desires from us, and this is the kind of service he promises to bless.

When Simon Peter said, 'Master, we have *toiled* all the night,' he used the same word (in verb form). When the Lord completed the long journey to Sychar where he encountered the woman of Samaria, it is recorded that he was *wearied* with his journey. The 'labouring' verb is used. It may therefore be used to describe a physically exhausting journey. It also appears in *John 4.38* to describe the heavy work of ploughing, and again in *Ephesians 4.28* to describe the work of a manual labourer or craftsman. Such passages help us to see the strenuous nature of biblical service for the Lord. Today, this term seems to have lost its force and challenge, for we imagine that Christian service can be as gentle as we want it to be.

When Paul tells us that our *labour* is not in vain in the Lord, he utters under inspiration a magnificent promise of God which will never be broken. The promise does not necessarily cover acts of Christian service which cost little and leave us fresh and vigorous. Our *mild* efforts are not guaranteed a blessing, nor are our *spasmodic* acts of service. Unfinished and abandoned projects may well turn out to be fruitless and unblessed. According to the promise it is our costly, tiring, taxing labour which will never be in vain in the Lord. If, therefore, we want to be certain to reap a blessing, our labour must qualify.

Paul uses this strong labouring word again in *1 Corinthians 3.8* when he says – 'Now he that planteth and he that watereth are one:

---

* 'The Greek signifies to be pressed, namely, with pains. It implies a diligent and hard labour. It will make a man take any pains, endure any toil, be it at any cost.' – William Gouge.

and every man shall receive his own reward according to his own *labour*.' The laborious activity of a farmer (in an age when sophisticated farm machinery did not exist) is considered a suitable metaphor for our work in the church.

Paul uses the term yet again in *Romans 16.6* where he speaks warmly of Mary – 'who bestowed much *labour* on us'. Mary went out of her way to do all manner of things for the messengers of God, and so Paul employs his favourite intensive-toil, labouring word.

Another example of this word being used to describe the service of ordinary believers occurs in *1 Thessalonians 1.2-3*, where Paul writes: 'We give thanks to God always for you all, making mention of you in our prayers; remembering without ceasing your work of faith, and *labour* of love.' Thessalonian believers toiled together for souls in such a way that Paul calls them 'ensamples' (or patterns) to other churches *(1 Thessalonians 1.7-8)*. Could our churches be viewed in this way? Could *my* participation be so warmly commended? Have I really grasped how great *my* contribution ought to be?

The tiring-toil term appears in a word of promise in *Hebrews 6.10*, where the writer says: 'For God is not unrighteous to forget your work and *labour* of love.' He will never lose sight of our strenuous efforts, and will both bless them and reward them. The question is – What do we do for the Lord which would cause him to take pleasure in us? What special burden do we bear for the cause of the Gospel? Or do we hold the view that the Christian life must always be easy and comfortable, and that we need only do things that give us a level of enjoyment untouched by pain or difficulty?

The writer of *Hebrews* goes on to say: 'And we desire that every one of you do shew the same diligence to the full assurance of hope unto the end: that ye be not slothful, but followers of them who through faith and patience inherit the promises.'

In these words we are reminded yet again that zealous participation in Christian service is not the duty of leaders only, but of all Christians. We also learn that tiring service is connected with the blessing of assurance, and that we must keep the flame of zeal burning to the very end of our journey. The heroes of faith of the Bible are realistic examples for us to follow. They were not an exceptional or unusual group of people, but a reasonable pattern for Christians in every age.

The writer of *Hebrews* has only one word for believers who opt out of the standard. They are, he says, *slothful,* which means slow, lazy and complacent. How many of us, though respected members of our churches, would fall under that description? May the Lord stir our hearts to yield our energies to his work!

The intensive-toil term, with its fatigue and, yes, even its pain, is essential to an adequate concept of the Christian life. We must not allow Satan to question, undermine or dilute the duty of vigorous commitment to Christian service, for we are called to be fellow-labourers in the Lord's work.

2. The striving-contending term

Paul switches to an entirely different labouring term in writing to the Philippians, and by this means he sheds further light on the lengths to which we must be prepared to go in our service for the Lord. Here, he uses a word which comes straight from the arena of conflict: the combative events of the great public games. In the following quotation note the words – *striving together.* These come from the Greek word *sunathleo,* which means to contend in partnership with others. (The Greek word *athleo* is the basis of the English word athlete.)

Paul urges – 'Only let your conversation be as it becometh the gospel of Christ: that whether I come and see you, or else be absent, I may hear of your affairs, that ye stand fast in one spirit, with one mind *striving together* for the faith of the gospel' *(Philippians 1.27).*

The athletic competitor is prepared to train hard and to suffer exhaustion for his sport. Once his bout or event is underway he is a man under compulsion, with no regard for his rights or comforts. Ready even to risk injury, he is utterly determined to complete the contest, and to win it if humanly possible. No other mental attitude could sustain him. This is true of athletes of every age, and this is the picture which Paul borrows to describe the Christian service commitment of every believer.

It would be unthinkable for a competitor in a key athletic event to suddenly walk off the track, change back into everyday clothes and head for home, just because it all seemed too much effort. Yet this is what happens all the time in today's 'arena' of Christian service. If the evening is damp or cold, Sunday School visitors may abandon their stage of the 'race' so that their absentees remain unvisited. Sometimes a church prayer meeting, quite unaccountably, will suffer a tired evening, as the Lord's athletes decide to act as spectators and take no personal part in the prayer effort. Sadder still, some members of the 'team' will not even turn up at the track.

'Oh, but I don't feel like praying,' complains many a contestant. The answer of the Lord is – 'Gird up the loins of your mind,' take yourself in hand; prepare your heart; summon your energies, and shoulder your share of responsibility in this life-and-death contest for souls. God requires us to regard our spiritual duties as though they were events in a global athletic contest. We *must* compete because we are *listed* to compete. It is *imperative* that we are in the place and in the event to which God has assigned us, and he will hold us accountable for our indiscipline and absenteeism.

The apostle's athletic analogy prompts us to compare ourselves with amateur athletes who may be seen jogging every morning, come wind, come weather, or visiting a training circuit three or four times a week. They commit themselves to an increasingly intensive programme as they approach the competition season. They are prepared to make sacrifices not only physically but also financially and socially. And yet, as Paul says, 'they do it to obtain a corruptible crown.' Will disciples of Christ show similar dedication to their cause? Will we, as church members, show the same single-mindedness? Is it possible that worldlings show greater devotion to their interests than we do to our Saviour?

We note again that Paul's exhortation to the Philippians is given to *every* Christian; to every church member. This is not only for ministers and missionaries. We are viewed as a whole – 'striving together', co-operating to advance the faith. Can we honestly say that we participate in Christian service activities in such a spirit? Are we ready to sustain fatigue, injury, and to forgo some comforts, and excessive leisure pursuits? If we are church leaders, have we sought to plan the activities of our church so that as many as desire to do so may have the opportunity to serve the Lord in a significant manner?

This biblical concept of service transcends all distinctions in the local church, whether between pastors and 'lay' people, or between men and women. We note how Paul, in *Philippians 4.3*, uses this contesting term in connection with women members: 'And I entreat thee also, true yokefellow, help those women which *laboured* with me *[the Greek here is – wrestled jointly with me]* in the gospel, with Clement also, and with other my fellowlabourers.'

How does our service for the Lord appear in the light of this striving-wrestling-contending term? If God's people everywhere took this word to heart (with all its implications), evangelical churches would be transformed overnight. No longer would Sunday Schools be tiny due to lack of helpers. No longer would streets go unvisited, or youth gatherings be understaffed. No longer would churches go uncleaned and Sunday School minibuses unserviced. What hives of activity our churches would all become, and how satisfied, fulfilled and assured the people of God would be. Also, God's people would be drawn closer together, because fellowship in service always brings about the deepest and best bonds.

3. The fighting term

In *Colossians 1.29* Paul uses another strong word, different from the previous one, yet also taken from the arena of public contest. Speaking of his preaching, he writes – 'Whereunto I also labour, *striving* according to his working.' The word translated *labour* is the term we considered first – the tiring-toil word. But the word *striving* in this particular verse is from the Greek, *agonizomai*, from which we get our English word 'agonising'. It means to fight, in the public arena, but with even more strenuous exertion than any of the previous terms. This word includes a 'do-or-die' element.

Paul uses this same verb when he speaks of competitors straining for supremacy in *1 Corinthians 9.25-27*, where one of the contestants is a boxer. In *1 Timothy 6.12*, he again uses this word when he exhorts Timothy to – '*fight* the good fight of faith.' He also uses it in *2 Timothy 4.7*, where he declares – 'I have *fought* a good fight.'

This *agonizomai* term therefore speaks of fighting for something, telling us that our Christian service will demand times of supreme effort. We are to be like athletes in the sense of being constantly in training and determined to do well, but we are also to be like gladiators, soldiers, wrestlers and other combative contestants, who are prepared to commit their last ounce of strength to avoid defeat and secure success.

Agonizomai sees the wrestler or athlete at the very climax of the bout or event, when the ultimate burst of effort is demanded for victory. The wrestler is now poised between victory and defeat; the runner must summon up the most intense concentration and determination to surge ahead over the last few metres.

This fighting verb tells us that we are to *finish* tasks we have begun for the Lord. We are to take full responsibility for projects, and to keep going when we are tempted to let things go. It may be that the believer is exceptionally tired and strained, but to be faithful to his Christian service commitment he must cast himself upon the Lord, and make a magnificent last effort. Are we prepared for this? The flesh may protest, and insist that this is reasonable once or twice in a lifetime, for degree finals, or moving house, but not for other times. The flesh will ask for ease and comfort, but the servant of the Lord should want to count for the Gospel and for the cause throughout this present, brief pilgrimage.

This fighting verb also calls to mind a military unit, which is just what the local church is, in spiritual terms. Are we prepared, for the

Lord's sake, to accept military conditions? Are we willing to accept modest rations as far as self-interest and personal pleasure are concerned? Will we yield up 'peacetime' comforts and privileges to make the battle for souls our chief interest and occupation?

Is our church on a battle footing? Or are we the kind of people who are unavailable for vital tasks, and who walk with relaxed and measured pace through their comfortable Christian lives? Are we the kind of young people who spend their energies chasing after leisure interests? Are we among those who are too self-serving to be found where the spiritual work is hard and demanding? Or are we unreliable, ready to start, but never willing to persist in any task?

Even worldlings do their duty to their nation in time of national peril. When war is declared, people in their millions accept the indignities and rigours of conscription, with its loss of liberty and leisure. The history of war records countless acts of selfless heroism and sacrifice, and all for an earthly cause, however noble. By contrast, the heavenly battle is often poorly served, because the soldiers of Christ fight merely as spare-time, peacetime, 'territorials'. The Christian battle is for them a secondary matter, in which 'home leave' takes precedence over the war, and comfort and security takes precedence over injury and inconvenience. Is this our kind of war?

We are followers of our Lord; he is our compelling example. Did not he labour and endure conflict to the end? The answer is given in *Luke 22.44* – 'And being in an agony he prayed more earnestly: and his sweat was as it were great drops of blood falling down to the ground.' It is significant that the Greek word used for our Lord's *agony* is a near neighbour of this contesting-fighting word which Paul uses to describe Christian service. Is our notion of Christian service in line with such a term?

How much blessing, assurance, instrumentality and spiritual happiness is forfeited by the Lord's people because they will not love him by yielding up their lives to his service! Christian service is a fight – a fight against the powers of darkness, the hardness of human hearts, and also against the indolence and lethargy *of our own bodies*. We must recognise what we are up against, and commit ourselves wholeheartedly to serve the Lord.

4. The aspiring-to-honour term

A very striking perspective on spiritual service is gained from a term used by the apostle in *2 Corinthians 5.9*. Reflecting on the imminence of death, he says – 'Wherefore we *labour,* that, whether present or absent, we may be accepted of him.' In this passage the word *labour* comes from a Greek term which speaks of aspiring to honour. Paul is saying that he labours to please the Lord to gain his commendation. He is driven by an ambition to achieve something significant for him. He builds for the last day, when all the ransomed shall be gathered with Christ in triumph, and all his glory will be revealed. Nothing thrills the heart of Paul more than to contribute to that day, the climax of all time, and to be approved by his Lord and King.

Paul uses the same term in *Romans 15.20*, saying – 'Yea, so have I strived *[aspired to the honour]* to preach the gospel, not where Christ was named.' We may paraphrase – 'I strained for the honour of preaching the Gospel where Christ had not previously been named.' The point is that for Paul, Christian service was a very great honour and privilege. It was his highest aim to accomplish glorious things. He laboured like a man passionately committed to a noble task, and with his eyes fixed on the commendation of his King.

Are we similarly dedicated to our Christian service? Will we sacrifice comforts and advantages for this greatest possible honour, the role of doing the Lord's work in our church? Will this dominate our schemes and come first in every way? This aspiring-to-honour term teaches us the true spirit of Christian service. A lesser attitude will fail to sustain the vigour and commitment which is due.

Other 'working church' texts and metaphors

Any lingering doubts that every church member is intended to take a part in the work of the local church should be dispelled by

Ephesians 4.11-12, once we understand how these verses are meant to be read. Paul writes –

> 'And he gave some, apostles; and some, prophets; and some, evangelists; and some, pastors and teachers; for the perfecting of the saints, for the work of the ministry, for the edifying of the body of Christ.'

This is the translation and punctuation of the *King James Version*. However, it is widely agreed that the correct sense of these words is only evident when the comma is removed after the word 'saints'. The verse then tells us that preachers are given in order to train the saints for the work of the ministry. In other words, it is the task of preachers to educate and prepare the entire flock for the work and witness of Christ. The *NASB* renders the passage in this way:

> 'And he gave some…as evangelists, and some as pastors and teachers, for the equipping of the saints for the work of service, to the building up of the body of Christ.'

The context confirms that this is how we should read this passage, for Paul goes on to define church growth and maturity as a process which involves every single part and component of the body (verse 16). Just as the human body grows as the result of intense biological activity in every part, so the local church grows by the involvement of every member.

Dr William Hendriksen, in his acclaimed commentary on *Ephesians*, writes:–

> 'The important lesson taught here is that not only apostles, prophets, evangelists, and those who are called "pastors and teachers", but the entire church should be engaged in spiritual labour. The universal priesthood of believers is stressed here…Church attendance should mean more than "going to hear the Rev. A." Unless, with a view to the service, there is adequate preparation, a desire for association, wholehearted *participation*, and the spirit of adoration, there is bound to be Sabbath-desecration. And during the week, too, every member should equip himself to be engaged in a definite ministry, whether that be imparting comfort to the sick, teaching, neighbourhood evangelisation, tract distribution, or whatever be the task for which one is especially

equipped. The meaning of *Ephesians 4.11-12* is, moreover, that it is the task of the officers of the church to equip the church for these tasks.'

The case for the total involvement of all church members in Christian service is confirmed over and over again in Scripture, but we shall rest with just two further texts which are clear and uncontroversial.

Paul again compares the local church to a human body needing all its organs, limbs and other parts in *1 Corinthians 12.11-12*. Members who appear to be of the least significance have nevertheless been placed in the church by Christ to play a vital part. Paul says –

> 'But now are they many members, yet but one body. And the eye cannot say unto the hand, I have no need of thee: nor again the head to the feet, I have no need of you. Nay, much more those members of the body, which seem to be more feeble, are necessary' *(1 Corinthians 12.20-22).*

We are told that God is determined to use the least conspicuous members of the fellowship to bring his purposes to pass. What blessing we therefore forfeit if we fail to encourage and train every member in Christian service, including the 'least'. In fact, Paul's words suggest that those who *seem* to be the lowliest members may well prove to be the most vital and fruitful for the church's advance. Perhaps some will turn out to be the best 'fishers' of others.

Yet another passage, *Romans 12.1-5*, should certainly challenge any who still draw back from the idea that *all* believers should be involved in the active work of their church. Note the full implications of Paul's words:

> 'I beseech you therefore, brethren, by the mercies of God, that ye present your bodies a living sacrifice, holy, acceptable unto God, which is your reasonable service.'

It is not enough to be a worshipper in prayer, song, and the hearing of the Truth, while offering no active service for the Lord. That is merely a partial sacrifice. Such an offering does not include one's energies and time to any great degree. It does not involve the surrender of much. It is often said that actions speak louder than words. The entire person must be offered, sincerely and energetically, to the Lord.

In the same passage Paul goes on to speak of the different aptitudes which are to be offered up. He then utters that ringing exhortation that we are to be—'fervent in spirit; *serving* the Lord' *(Romans 12.11)*. With so many challenges along these lines, how can true believers remain unconvinced about the principle that all are to be deeply involved in the work and service of the congregation? How can we remain uninvolved in the ministry and labour of our church?

Do we need further scriptural proof of the concept of the working church? All the famous church metaphors bear out this teaching. The New Testament uses the illustration of the Temple under construction to depict a growing, evangelising church. This increases in size in such a way that every column, beam and wall is utilised in the support of the total structure. Every component plays a part. Other church metaphors also honour the 'working church' principle. The picture of the flock of sheep reminds us that the reproduction of lambs is spread through the entire flock.

What has gone wrong?

A few years ago the writer heard of a small congregation in which a number of members became convicted about their lack of participation in Christian work, and began to clamour for avenues of service. However, events proved that they had more light than their church officers on the true character of the Christian life. The pastor and elders recoiled away from their new-found zeal, dismissing it as superficial activism.

Often the situation is the other way about, and pastors and leaders cannot persuade the members to offer themselves in the service of the Lord, and so recapture the activity and the atmosphere of those New Testament churches.

It must be admitted, however, that sometimes it is the minister who has drifted from the time-honoured track. An article once appeared in an evangelical periodical which was aimed at comforting the average married woman in church membership. The author, a pastor, had apparently received complaints from such a person that there was nothing for her to do in the church. 'I am only a very ordinary person,' she had said. 'I cannot preach or do any significant things. I am consigned to shopping and housework. How can I feel happy and fulfilled?'

The article set out to explain to this lady, and all in her position, that she should not aspire to great things. After all, she had her family to bring up, and she also had the opportunity for a ministry of prayer. Were these not enough for her?

It is certainly true that raising a family is a highly significant ministry, and so is the work of private prayer. But the answer given to this reasonable question was hardly adequate, suggesting that the author had little awareness of his own responsibility to lead and train the entire membership into Christian service, in accordance with *Ephesians 4.11-12*. His questioner was miserable and unfulfilled because there was nothing for her to do in her church, and perhaps her pastor was partially responsible for that. He had not realised, and nor had his elders or deacons, that they should have been prayerfully planning soul-seeking activities for their church to undertake.

There is so much to be done, and there is so much that women members can do better than men. The most obvious example is that of child evangelism. If only evangelical churches today would carry on the tradition of the past by drawing *large* numbers of children and teenagers from the community for Sunday School and Bible Class, they would soon find the gifts of women members fully employed along with those of the men. And large Sunday Schools need not only teachers, but also helpers, pianists, visitors, and collectors and drivers, if they are to cater for large numbers of children. In these days we must collect the young if we are to succeed. How can this be done, if pastors and their people do not believe in the obligation of Christian service? There is a full workload waiting for both men and women in our churches, if only we would recognise the needs.

What has happened to the Sunday School vision? Why do so many churches take no responsibility for the rising generation in their town? Why are they content to leave them at the mercy of an unbelieving and godless society? If we could only restore a right concept of regular Christian service as a duty of all believers, such ministries would flourish again, as in years gone by.

Why have we drifted so far from the 'working church' concept of the New Testament? This was, after all, the standard of most Bible-believing churches up until roughly the 1950s. This writer remembers the time when the average Bible-believing church encouraged everyone to serve the Lord. If you did not, you were virtually a second-class Christian. But because most did so, a church of 150 members could operate a Sunday School of 300-400, plus a full programme of weeknight activities and devotionals. The children's department was a good measure of how well the people served, because it has always been a 'labour-intensive' ministry. But believers engaged in many other avenues of service also.

Why have things changed? One answer is that this precious working church concept has ceased to be clearly articulated and pressed upon the Lord's people, so that they no longer have an adequate view of the nature of a local church, and the duties of her members.

Secondly, as we have noted, leaders of churches have sometimes neglected to organise avenues of service for the members. Indeed, some have been decidedly reluctant to complicate and burden their own lives with this further responsibility.

Thirdly, a poor example has sometimes been set by the more established, middle-aged members of churches, who have themselves had no specific avenues of service, and no intention of seeking them. To make matters worse, such people have often held office in the church as elders or deacons. Nothing could be more likely to give younger members the impression that Christian service is merely an option.

Fourthly, we must point the finger at our natural tendency to laziness, and our aversion to hard work. When a church needs a cleaning workparty it is usually easy to guess which members will not be available. Whatever the need within a church, there are some who will always make themselves scarce. The unfought sin of lethargy is a great enemy to the working church concept.

Fifthly, some believers fail to make a worthwhile commitment in Christian service because they are ruled by muddle. Such friends are not necessarily lazy, but their lives are so badly organised that every moment of their time is wholly occupied with personal and domestic activities, and none is left for the things of the Lord. We have a duty to order our priorities with great care, exercising self-discipline in the use of time.

A sixth reason why some believers miss the mark in Christian service is because they pander to the desires of the flesh, giving themselves generous helpings of leisure, recreational activity, trips away from home, visits to various friends and relatives, holidays, and so on. Some even become television addicts; some read too much; and some decorate and redecorate their homes with fastidious care. Whatever the 'excess', the result is that they have no time for serious Christian service.

A seventh reason for non-involvement in Christian service is the low level of *feeling* possessed by some believers. They seem not to care about the health and vigour of their church, let alone the souls of the lost. Some seem oblivious to the things which need to be done. They would not mind (or so it would seem) if the church never sought or won a soul, adult or child, all year long. They would feel no pain if the Sunday School ran down to zero, or the flow of unsaved visitors to the evangelistic preaching service dried up altogether. They probably would not mind if the church lingered for years on the edge of closure. Nothing, absolutely nothing, would stir *them* to volunteer for the service of the Lord.

Are we not committed to the Lord's work? Do we see ourselves in any of the reasons for failure just reviewed? If so, we are missing the central purpose of our being left briefly in this world as ambassadors of the Lord. We are also missing the greatest spiritual joys, for these flow especially to those who *serve* the Lord and not themselves. We should never lose sight of the great promise of *Isaiah 54*, where the joy of the church is firmly rooted in evangelistic labour and the blessing of spiritual parentage.

Vulnerable to error

Wherever churches neglect the involvement of all members, they become exposed to unsound and harmful 'isms', which are numerous. For example, many believers during the last half-century, instinctively aware that something was missing in their inactive churches, began to yearn for spiritual excitement and fulfilment. The result is that they fell prey to the charismatic movement, with its bustling pursuit of new phenomena, and its claim to have rediscovered spiritual experiences neglected for centuries. Countless unfulfilled Christians have turned in this direction to fill the void within.

Needless to say, the charismatic movement has not led them into meaningful labour for the Lord, because it substitutes for real Christian service the imagined exercise of spiritual gifts such as prophecy, healing, tongues, revelations, and focuses so much energy on 'spiritual' entertainment. The irony is that a lazy or uncommitted Christian may be a very happy charismatic. This is not to say that all charismatics are lazy or uninvolved in Christian work, but because the movement emphasises so-called spiritual gifts, a massive and self-serving cult of experience-seeking emotionalism and worldly entertainment-style music has emerged, which has little in common with the unselfish service of Christ.

A working church has the capacity!

We often hear believers say, 'If only we could get the Gospel on to a leading secular television channel.' But would this be as valuable as we might hope? Supposing we obtained a good programme opportunity just once in a while. It would certainly not be shown at peak viewing hours, and the percentage of people who would see it might be very small.

Such an opportunity would certainly be valued by believers, but do we appreciate the powerful opportunities already in our grasp? We are not dependent on the hope of occasional mention on major media facilities, when we can easily put the equivalent of several programmes round every house in our neighbourhood every year in the form of good evangelistic literature and doorstep conversations. A working church has the capacity for such ventures, not for one week a year, but for most weeks of the year. Good-sized teams may comb a district, supported by the fervent prayers of all, and God will be sure to bless them, in his time.

Paul's words about labouring for the Lord embrace a whole range of activities including teaching, witnessing, caring for people and visiting homes. The Jewish leaders complained in fury to the apostles, 'Behold, ye have filled Jerusalem with your doctrine.' We should be doing the same in our communities.

So many activities are possible for a working church. Can a church give greater financial support for preachers, evangelists, missionaries, or for evangelistic literature or special ventures at home? The average evangelical congregation today is not large, and if the church is to provide for such expenditure, many practical jobs will need to be undertaken by the members in order to save money. Who is available to help with the cleaning and repairs and redecorations? A church which answers to the church metaphors of the Bible is a hive of activity in which everyone takes a share, willingly accepting rotas and other arrangements designed to ensure a fair distribution of the tasks to be covered.

The Lord observes our works

Have we lost sight of the fact that the Lord knows and marks our *accomplishments* or *works*? When Christ says to the Laodiceans, 'I know thy works,' he refers to the commitment of the entire church, not just that of the minister or office bearers. Their accomplishments were their collective and individual duty. Their doctrinal standard or constitution was not under discussion, but their deeds and accomplishments were.

Although the Laodiceans were not altogether cold, neither were they fervent. The best description we can use for the church members of Laodicea, is that they were 'pedestrian' or 'low-key', and lacking in any costly toil for the Master. One day we must stand before God to give account of our time on earth, perhaps as office bearers or as preachers. We shall face the Lord and tell him what we did with his precious, blood-bought people. Did we allow a local detachment of the King's Own Army to become indisciplined, indifferent, self-serving, unapplied, unused and unfulfilled?

Surely this is the first and most vital objective for the present time – to re-establish the standards of sacrificial, committed Christian living. May the Lord move us to turn away from the pursuit of too-lovely homes, easy lifestyles, worldly fulfilment, and excessive leisure, to begin lives of genuine dedication in the costly, and yet wonderful, service of the Lord. We must realise that the Word urges holy activism and zealous labour for the Lord. We are called to be imitators of the apostle, who said, 'We then, as workers together with him, beseech you also that ye receive not the grace of God in vain.'

The Lord uses our efforts

Our zeal must be based on the realisation that no great Gospel work can be done without human instrumentality. Too many Christians today have come to think that the pulpit proclamation of the Word is all that is necessary. They accept that the Lord uses 'means' to the extent that he requires the Gospel to be preached, but not to bring the people under the sound of the Gospel. The Lord, they seem to think, will do all that himself. There is no hope for our churches unless we can successfully counter such ideas.

In recent years there has been a renewal of interest in studying great preachers of the past, particularly those who were revival instruments. We have rejoiced to have biographies available of Whitefield, Jonathan Edwards, Spurgeon and others, but Christian people often take the wrong attitude to such revival instruments. Their attitude is, 'Oh, if only we could have preachers like this today! If only we could have another George Whitefield! If only we had men upon whom the Spirit would come, so that great things could happen.' The mistake here is that people have failed to notice that in times of revival *all* believers labour in witness, no matter what the cost. People see only the glory and success, and fail to notice how both the preachers and their supporters were stretched and exhausted by the rigours of revival.

How wonderful, people think today, if half a dozen revival instruments could secure all the blessing by proxy, as it were, and turn Britain upside-down. Our souls would be thrilled beyond measure at mighty events. We would be the most blessed spectators in the world. Is not revival God-sent? Is it not a demonstration of sovereignty? Of course it is, but God still uses human instruments, even in revival, to convince the masses.

As soon as we talk about dedicated activity we hear some saying that it is our responsibility to be *faithful* not *fruitful*, which is too often a way of justifying a low-key approach to Christian service. 'Faithfulness', in this context, tends to mean jogging along at a slow and comfortable pace.

However, the inspired penmen of the Bible use terms such as *labour*, and *toil*, and *striving*. May the Lord stir our hearts, so that we shall return to the old standard of total, sacrificial commitment to the Lord! May we desire first the kingdom of God in our lives! May we learn once again to walk the old paths of burning activity in our fellowships. No other policy will prove the power of God and bring down the high privilege of soul-saving instrumentality. And no other approach to the Christian life will bring down the blessings of assurance, joy and peace so much as this one. May the words of an old, well-loved hymn be our prayer:

> *I would not, Lord, with swift-winged zeal*
>   *On this world's errands go,*
> *And labour up the heavenly hill*
>   *With weary feet and slow.*
>
> *O not for thee my weak desires,*
>   *My poorer, baser part!*
> *O not for thee my fading fires,*
>   *The ashes of my heart!*
>
> *O grant me in my golden time,*
>   *A zealous servant's part;*
> *For thee the glory of my prime,*
>   *The fulness of my heart!*